THE MISTAKES OF A *Woman* VOL 2

NEW BEGINNINGS
M. SOSA

First Printing, 2017

ISBN: 978-0-9951533-5-6

"Letting go is hard but holding on to the *wrong person* is even harder."

CONTENTS

DEDICATION

This book is dedicated to *everybody that's ever been through a heartbreak, is currently going through one* and *to those who are having a hard time letting go*. I hope my words help heal some of your wounds, and help guide you towards a greater sense of happiness. I hope, after you've finished this book, that a part of the weight you're carrying has been lifted.

INTRODUCTION

"I was deeply in love with you. It blinded me. I became the woman I feared most by accepting the love I was given, and not the love I *wanted* and *deserved*. I made excuses for you, and gave you one too many chances, even though you didn't deserve them. I put your needs before my own but enough was enough... I was taking my power back and making myself a priority. I wasn't going to tolerate you breaking me down any further. I was going to build myself back up by *loving myself* with the same love I had given you."

CHAPTER 1
Goodbye To My Past Relationships

"My mistake was letting you come back into my life, each time you needed me. You'd be good for the first few weeks, then you'd mess things up, and leave again... *leaving me* even more broken than the last time. I had nobody to blame but myself for letting you back in so easily. I had to learn to say *goodbye* and actually mean it."

It's never an easy step to take when a relationship ends. You feel overwhelmed because you're not sure how to function without the person you're accustomed to. Things you used to do together, are now things you must do alone... and that can be quite frightening for some.

While some of us can let go and move on from past relationships, others tend to remember how their ex *used to make them feel*. They reminisce on all the good times, not the bad ones and that's why many people have a hard time letting go. They're stuck on who that person used to be instead of accepting who they truly are and probably always were. Their mask finally came off but it's still not enough because they're stuck in denial of what is happening in the present. They keep reliving the past, overthinking what *could have been*.

We hold on to past relationships for several reasons which stop us from facing reality and stop us from living our lives.

You feel you'll never meet someone new or it may take too long to find love again

One of the reasons we stay stuck is because we feel we'll never find someone new that will understand us the same way our ex did.

I remember when my ex and I broke up. I felt as if my whole world was falling apart and no other man would ever compare to him. He knew the music I loved, knew the types of movies I disliked, knew my friends, knew the things that turned me on but also knew the things that would tick me off. The thought of us no longer being together made me feel as if it would take me forever to meet someone who would *understand me*, like he did.

Your worth is not defined by who loves you

Another reason we have a hard time letting our past go is because we base our self-worth on who loves us. If you believe that "being dumped" or being single makes you unworthy, you are completely wrong. You're perceiving the breakup as a reflection of your worth as a person. But why? Most people with low self-esteem associate a failed relationship with failure, while someone with a boost of self-confidence will feel happy of being free of a toxic relationship.

Feeling as if you can't move on from a past relationship is you not accepting that your ex is simply *not the right one for you*. You overthink every possible scenario to why you can't live without them, when the reality is, you believe you're not *good enough* for anybody else in the world, except your ex. Which means you're denying yourself of finding real love because you're too busy believing you're not good enough for love... and we know that's not the case. You're worthy of it all.

Never lose yourself when loving someone. YOUR dreams and YOUR goals matter too. I'm not saying there's a line that shouldn't be crossed. And when you know you're giving more than you should, it might be time to take a step back and realize where you're standing.

You feel guilty and haven't forgiven yourself

Feeling guilty can also hinder the process of completely letting go. If you feel you did something wrong during your past relationships, such as using your partner for money or used them to get over someone else, you may feel the need to make amends.

If you feel you hurt them and there's something within you that's left unsaid, maybe it's a sign you should be making an apology or asking for forgiveness. I'm not saying you necessarily need to speak with them, but you need to figure out what you can do to make yourself feel better. It could even mean just writing an apology letter, reading it out loud to yourself and burning it.

You might also feel as if you made the biggest mistake of your life by letting your ex go, or maybe you said something you shouldn't have said when breaking up. Either way, you shouldn't be blaming yourself for anything you've done or you'll keep believing that if you had done things differently, you wouldn't feel all the pain you're in right now. If you go down that road, you'll only find more grief and you'll never feel the need to move on with your life.

Keep reminding yourself that everybody makes mistakes, and that includes you. The only way to feel love with someone new is by loving yourself and forgiving yourself for anything that might have gone wrong in the past.

To give and receive love, you must be able to love yourself unconditionally, which means forgiving yourself for any wrongdoings and things you cannot change.

You haven't wasted your time

I used to believe whenever one of my relationships ended, that it was time wasted, time I could never get back. For that reason, I would despise whoever I was with because I felt I had given them the world, while they were busy thinking about themselves.

But the truth is, all the time I spent with one person was never time wasted because I had to remind myself of all the things I did accomplish during that time. So, I reminded myself that I had built great friendships and had also furthered my career. The moment I shifted my focus on all the positive I had done, instead of the negative, I realized it wasn't time wasted after all.

Thinking in such a positive way empowered me, and it stopped me from victimizing myself. It made me realize that everything I've been through is what catapulted me to where I am now. It prepared me for a life full of opportunities, for happiness and especially growth.

You expected them to be what you wanted

One reason, that I can honestly admit I've been guilty of a couple of times, is when we fall in love with the romance we once felt and the excitement of how they once made us feel. The fact that those memories create such an imprint in our minds fascinates me because it shows how anything that captures our hearts has the possibility of staying with us forever. It also shows how we're able of creating unrealistic expectations of how we want the future to be.

When you expect your partner to do things he may never be able to do, you create illusions in your mind of how you *believe* he might someday be. But it isn't how he is now, and he might never be at the level you expect him to be, so you're creating a fake persona in which you hold onto for years, maybe even decades.

You're holding on to *hope* that *someday,* he will turn into the person you expect him to be, and that makes it a lot harder to let go.

You keep comparing yourself to others

I remember being in this predicament, wondering why I couldn't be happily married or in love with the man of my dreams. While my girlfriends were busy living their lives, married or celebrating an anniversary, I was single and alone… feeling down and out over my breakup. Comparing myself to them was a constant reminder of *him*. It felt like everybody around me was in a committed relationship while I was out here looking for love. When you start comparing yourself to others, you start to feel as if you're in a lower category than them and if you don't meet the same requirements as them, you feel worthless.

All you're doing is creating an unhappy place in your head that makes you believe you *can't* be happy if you're not involved with someone, so you keep feeling sorry for yourself and end up reminiscing on how things used to be with your ex. Stop.

You simply don't want to let the past go

Just because you tell someone they should move on and they find it hard to do so, doesn't mean they don't want to.

What many people do is compare what you're saying to them to what they're feeling. They're fighting with themselves and debating if they should let go or keep holding on. A part of them wants to let go, but another part of them feels if they push their ex out of their lives completely that they will lose everything they ever had with them.

The truth is, the relationship is already lost so all they are doing is experiencing inner conflict that prevents them from living and carrying on with their lives.

You're listening to your heart instead of listening to your head

I can guarantee you that a good percentage of us have done this on several occasions. Our mind is telling us to let go while our heart is doing the opposite. It's as if our heart only wants to remember the *good times* and ignores everything that is happening in the present.

You hold on because you believe it's the right thing to do since you share a history with this person, and you believe deep down within that they are the ones that will hold your heart forever… but you're lying to yourself because all it is doing is causing you more harm than good. That pain you're feeling is the pain of not being able to *let go*.

You're fantasizing about them

It's happened to me on a few occasions where I relived old memories and imagined my ex in my life. I didn't want to let go so I imagined him still being around me.

I pictured us happy, like we used to be. I created a fantasy because facing reality was out of the question. It felt good to fantasize about how things could have turned out, and I even imagined being back together with him, living the life I should have. But the problem with fantasizing is that it can only make you feel good for so long. Eventually, even if you're not willing to face reality, you'll have no choice but to do so. I know it isn't easy to accept.

You're hanging on to hope

I've been there, letting the same person back into my life every time they needed me. Now, this is something that I struggled with for years. I kept hanging on to hope that someday, somehow, my ex would come back into my life. I kept believing that he would somehow knock on my door and profess his undying love for me... but that obviously never happened. It happens in movies and in soap operas but rarely does it happen in real life and that was something that I had to live with.

There's a point where you should accept the blame for letting them back in so easily and you have to learn to say goodbye for good, or you'll keep reliving the same situation over and over, heartbreak after heartbreak.

It's not easy to let go of someone you feel attached to but ending all contact with them is essential for growth. While you may feel that letting go of that hope is ruining your chances at finding love again, it's quite the opposite to say the least. You will find love again and *you won't spend the rest of your life alone*. You will create new friendships that may lead to something serious but one thing you won't be is *alone*. Letting go of that hope opens your chances of meeting the *right one*, if you forgive yourself and open yourself up to the many possibilities waiting for you.

Sometimes losing people is part of life. As much as we want them, we've got to accept that they might not want us back. Accepting it is the toughest thing you will have to do but once you do, you'll see things a lot clearer.

Letting go of past relationships is HEALTHY. This is how you find peace of mind again. Holding on is an emotional torture nobody deserves, all you're doing is holding on because that is all you're familiar with but wouldn't you rather feel peace? Stop suffering by waiting for something that may never happen. It's causing you to obsess over someone that isn't even thinking of you that way. Give yourself the greatest gift by moving forward.

CHAPTER 2
No More Anger

"I'm not bitter anymore. I don't react when someone mentions your name. I live my life with *peace of mind* and no longer let anger consume it."

One of the mistakes we commonly make when trying to move on with our lives is holding on to anger and bitterness towards the person that hurt us. Revenge comes into play because we want them to suffer through a similar situation so they can understand the pain they put us through.

Yet, we ignore the fact that anger and bitterness are only weighing us down from moving forward. I remember my ex ending our relationship as if it meant nothing, and all I could think of was "how am I going to f**k him over so he feels the pain I felt?". I was in a dark place back then, and believed the only way to make someone understand how much they hurt me was by trying to inflict the same pain onto them.

It took me a while to realize that all that anger was only hurting me in the process. Think of it this way, if all you do is focus your energy on what they did to break your heart, all you're really doing is holding on to unnecessary baggage that is preventing you from moving on.

Stop trying to understand all the reasons behind

your heavy heart and why things didn't work out the way you expected them to, and start focusing on how you're going to make your life better. You deserve so much more than dwelling on anger that keeps making you unhappy.

The grief of losing someone usually pulls us down because we feel lost, confused, lonely and a variety of different emotions all at once. But once we start feeling anger, this is where we can jeopardize our future by doing things that can hurt us in the long run.

I've been able to move past these feelings by following a few simple steps.

Feel the pain. Feel it fully.

We harbor many emotions during a breakup and we often make the mistake of suppressing them so deep within that we forget to let them all out eventually.

They consume us. They take over our lives and affect us daily because we don't allow ourselves to feel it fully. Before you can let go of any emotion, you must allow yourself to feel everything to the core.

Doing this will help you express your feelings, and will also avoid you affecting other people around you that didn't inspire your anger. Let's keep it real, you don't want your emotions to burst out on the wrong people, right?

As much as it will hurt you to face what you're feeling, it will help you in the long run to face reality head on. And remember, anger hurts you more than the person who made you feel that way.

Express your anger to the person that hurt you

It's never an easy task to face the person that hurt you but it's one of the ways that may help you move on. You might be harbouring questions that haven't been answered or you might have many things you'd like to tell them. Expressing yourself is a great way of letting the other person know, they hurt you and you didn't deserve it.

But remember, *you can't control how that person will react* or the outcome of the conversation, so keep that in mind when speaking with them. The only thing you can control is how you express yourself. Yelling and screaming won't help a bit. The best way is to have a mature conversation and express all the emotions you felt during the breakup and all the frustrations you've been going through after it. You don't necessarily need to let them know everything you're feeling but expressing the main issues will help you with your anger.

OR

If you're not able to speak with them, take an object (a pillow, a stress ball, a tennis ball, etc) and express your anger vocally and feel free to use it physically if needed.

After one of my breakups, I recall taking my pillow and taking out my anger on it. I yelled and punched it several times, but at the end of it, I felt better. I exhaled, and you know what? It felt damn good! A part of me felt like it was my ex, and I was taking out all my frustrations on him by telling him exactly what he had done to me, but the physical part is what helped the most. I got so tired out from punching the pillow that I couldn't stop laughing afterwards. I realized that most of the anger I was holding in had been lifted. Silly way of getting rid of such an emotion but it worked!

Stop giving away your power

When you're mad, your focus is the person that made you feel that way. You focus on what they did and why they did it. Chances are you might also focus on what you could have done better, but you're spending too much time overthinking all the negative things instead of focusing on letting all that anger go. The longer you stay upset, the more power you're giving the person that upset you. You can either create your own happiness by accepting that you can't change what has happened or you can stay upset and let it ruin your happiness.

You choose.

CHAPTER 3
Overthinking…
Overanalyzing

"I'll never regret meeting you. You were the best mistake I ever made. All the tears I shed, all the time I lost, and the overthinking I did weren't in vain because they taught me to never give my love out so freely ever again. See, I learned to forgive those that have done me wrong in the past. So, I *thank you* for everything you put me through. You helped me grow. You helped me build the woman I am today and remind me of the type of woman I'll *never be again*."

I said this in *Volume 1* but I'll say it again. You cannot force someone to love you. If they're into you, you will know it with *their actions, not by their words*. We sometimes tend to stress over situations that are out of our control.

When someone leaves us, we stress over where it all went wrong or what we could have done to change the outcome. If I had done *this* or *that* differently, things might be different. We worry about things that we can't change because we figure the longer we obsess over the same situation, we'll somehow, hopefully, find the answer. It's a constant stress on our brain that leads to absolutely nothing.

I spent years questioning why things went wrong with one of my exes, and all it did was make me bitter and unhappy. I relived the breakup over and over instead of focusing on the present. It's as if someone else kept taking over my mind because even if I hung out with friends or pursued a new passion, I kept going back to our breakup.

I wanted to forget it all but I couldn't because I kept overanalyzing why things went wrong, instead of letting it go and accepting that he was no longer coming back. I was too consumed on focusing on *him*, instead of focusing on ME.

If you take the time to focus on yourself and focus on being a better version of you, you won't spend so much time trying to figure out answers to questions you might never be able to answer. It's like creating a problem that doesn't exist, and obsessing over how to solve it.

You're playing games with yourself. Think about it this way, at the beginning of any relationship, you start to wonder when he will commit to you. You start overthinking if he cares, if he wants to be with you, or if he's taking you seriously. Once he commits, you start worrying about when he's going to say, "I love you". And once that occurs, you start worrying about moving in together or even getting married. Then comes the issue if he'll cheat on you, and who he will cheat with. Is he satisfied? Is he happy? *Is he… is he… is he…* you waste valuable time asking yourself tons of questions *for nothing*.

Once you begin to overanalyze everything going on around you, it becomes a vicious cycle that is sometimes hard to get out of. But don't get me wrong, it's normal to have insecurities and wonder where your relationship is heading. The problem is when you overthink every little situation, *you forget to live*.

I recall going through this with one of my exes. Everything started out great and as the months went by, our relationship started suffering through trials and tribulations. He felt I was too needy and I felt he didn't give me enough attention. He ended things with me without a valid reason, so I constantly felt my mind wandering, overthinking and overanalizing the things that were said, why they were said and if I could have changed something if I had done things differently.

I couldn't understand where we went wrong or why things turned out the way they did. All I could do is reminisce on all the little details of our relationship, as if I had missed out on something important.

When a breakup occurs, you tend to wonder about all the possibilities that may still exist.

Does he still think about you? Will he ever come back again? Does he still love you? And the list goes on and on... The truth is, most relationships would function if people would stop overthinking and would start communicating. Say what's on your mind.

Stressing yourself out about your worries and fears is destructive. Once you stop, you start to breathe again and start to live life the way you should have. There's no point in dwelling in situations that cannot be changed or situations that are out of your control. Stop obsessing, overthinking and overanalizing. You owe it to yourself to be happy and to have peace of mind.

CHAPTER 4
Let Go
Of Regret

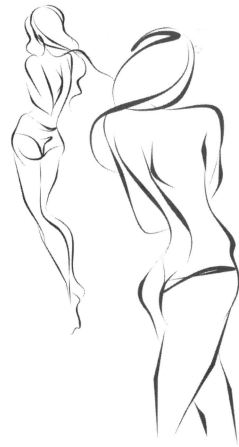

"Not everything is meant to be.
Sometimes, letting a bad relationship
go opens the door for the
right one to find you."

When a relationship ends, you feel the necessity to know what you did wrong or what you could have done to prevent the breakup. You overthink every little situation, in hopes that something will give you the answer you're looking for. On the contrary, all you're doing is being counterproductive by rehashing the past. The longer you dwell on the breakup and the "what if's", the longer you'll keep suffering.

Every time you revisit the past, you go back to that moment in time where you were happy and in a good place. When you should be focusing on what is going on in the present and the lessons you can learn from the mistakes you've made. Focus on all the good things going on in your life, like the people that are trying to support you. It's refreshing to vent about the way you're feeling, but remind yourself that it's also harmful to keep dwelling on it.

I'm not telling you to forget and not talk about it. I'm telling you that it's okay to talk about your problems so you can gain new insight from people who have your best interest at heart, but that doesn't mean it will work. In other words, you might feel the urge to keep dwelling on the past if you keep talking about it consistently. The less you talk about it every day, the more you'll realize you're in control of your well-being.

I've been there too, wishing I could turn back the clock and turn everything around. I kept wondering if I had done things differently, maybe we wouldn't be going through this breakup, or maybe we'd be getting married. That agonizing feeling of regret consumed me. I kept feeling if I had done more, I could have prevented the breakup... *but that wasn't true.*

All the sleepless nights I went through, feeling as if I messed everything up, were for nothing. I couldn't change what happened even though my heart kept telling me otherwise. I felt the need to blame myself.

I wallowed in self-pity for months because all I could feel was regret of not being able to change things. The fact that I wanted perfect closure kept me stuck until I realized that I had the power to stay in the same predicament day in, day out or I could free myself from all the pain by forgiving myself. I gave myself the closure I needed by accepting there was nothing more I could do to change the outcome. It was over and I couldn't keep blaming myself for it.

I started focusing my energy on the positive things going on in my life, instead of focusing on my regrets about what happened in my past relationship. I put my focus on my work and my writing, giving myself something to be proud about. Making sure that I could do something positive with my life and not worry about what could have been. I allowed myself to be happy again by changing my focus away from what I lost. I reclaimed pieces of myself that I had lost while I was in a relationship.

I also used affirmations daily to get through the painful memories. I reminded myself that every time I would regret a certain situation, I would repeat to myself one of the positive affirmations I had written down on a piece of paper.

Repeating these daily helped me through those dark times. It wasn't easy because the pain of losing someone is sometimes hard to bare but reading these affirmations helped me keep focus on the important things going on in my life.

Here are some of those affirmations:

"I was always enough, and if we're no longer together, it wasn't meant to be."

"Everything happening now
is for the best."

"Better days are coming,
I will be okay."

Anytime I had moments of regrets, I would remind myself that nothing is permanent.

Regardless of what I did in the past, I wouldn't allow anxiety to take over my body. I know you're probably thinking that it's not that easy to not live in regret but trust me when I say, you will overcome this and once you do, you will see life differently. You won't feel as though your whole world is crashing down.

No matter if you feel you did something you shouldn't have or could have done something better, the fact remains that *you are human* and you make mistakes like everybody else.

Sometimes losing someone opens the door to something better.

Switching everything from negative to positive is a great way to deal with regret as well. If you take the time to analyze your situation and open your eyes to the possibility that everything that happened was for the better, you may find it easier to let things go.

I realized this when I kept holding on to toxic relationships and friendships because I thought that's all I deserved, until the day came where I decided to stop *sacrificing myself* and *my happiness* for others. I had to cleanse my life to create space for something better. And the only way to do that was by not living in regret, but living in the present and accepting that certain things just *weren't meant to be*.

Keep reminding yourself that everything in life happens for a reason and that eventually, you will let go and move on. You're strong, smart and capable of standing tall again. Nothing will break you down because you've endured too much already. So, you lost someone that meant the world to you... sh*t happens. You're better off without them. It's important to remember that your life isn't over and you're still able to change your life around. You're able to try again but wiser than the last.

Feeling lonely might bring up these feelings of regret. You miss him, you miss how he made you feel and you wish he was still by your side. But those same feelings may also fool you into staying in a relationship way too long that isn't going to work out in the end.

If you find yourself in this situation, I would suggest waiting a while and thinking hard before picking up the phone to call your ex. Chances are things might work out but you'll have to do major work to make things right, but there's also a chance that things might take a turn for the worse. So be ready to face whatever comes your way.

One of the most important things to ask yourself is if you had your ex back in your life, would things be different or would you still be dealing with the same issues that caused the breakup? When you answer this honestly, you might find yourself fighting back and forth with your heart and your mind. But the right answer will spare you from another breakup.

CHAPTER 5
Don't Neglect Yourself

"You're beautiful, and even though he left you, doesn't mean you shouldn't shine. Fix that hair. Put on some makeup. Paint those nails. Strap on some heels.
It's time to think about *YOU*."

No matter how things ended, don't let yourself go. Don't neglect yourself. It's a shame to see women and men neglecting themselves after their heart has been torn to shreds. I've seen many of my female friends stop working out or even stop shaving because they didn't feel "beautiful" anymore, so there was no point in taking care of themselves like they used to.

While I understand there is sadness that consumes you, it's not okay to let go of the habits you once worked so hard to maintain. You shouldn't feel as though your whole world revolves solely on who you were with, because you are still someone important with or without them. Letting go of yourself will make you feel worthless and that's not the way anybody wants to feel after a breakup.

I've learned throughout the years that a breakup should be your motivation to make an even bigger effort to keep yourself uplifted and rejuvenated, no matter what it takes. During one of my breakups, I remember feeling down and out. My comfort was food and I ate ice cream, day in and day out because it made me feel good. But, after a few weeks, I realized none of my clothes fit the way they used to, so it was time for me to stop feeling sorry for myself and start focusing on becoming the happy, go-lucky, same old me.

I hit the gym at 6 a.m., five to six days a week. I was disciplined and knew that if I let myself go again, it would be even tougher the next time around to lose any of the weight I gained. So, I stayed consistent. I worked out for a couple of months and realized that the gym had become my boyfriend.

I know, it sounds silly but the truth is, the gym was my scapegoat. Instead of feeling sorry for myself, I learned to love myself unconditionally by doing things that made ME happy. And working out was something I enjoyed doing before my breakup, so getting back in tip top shape was a way for me to reward myself.

Now, the gym might not be your salvation but it can be the smallest gestures that make you smile, such as putting on a little makeup. Sometimes, we look like sh*t after someone leaves us because our eyes are puffy and our face looks pale. Why not brighten things up by going out and trying new shades of makeup on? Or even better, why not just head out to a spa and pamper yourself? It's the smallest things that make us realize what we've been missing out on.

While many of us wallow in our own self-pity when our hearts are broken, you should remember that YOU MATTER and picking yourself back up shows the world that you are ready to fight for your happiness. Remember, being comfortable is one thing, but looking as if a truck ran over you is something else. When you look as if you've given up hope, it's time to step your game up and fix yourself.

Having unkempt hair and nails are signs that you just don't care how you look anymore. There's nothing worse than seeing someone letting themselves go when they used to be the same ones that loved to impress others. If you used to do your nails at the salon, GO DO THEM. If you used to get your hair done, GO DO IT. If you used to hit the gym consistently, GO DO IT.

All the "used to's" should be things you should start doing again, or you're basically telling yourself you don't think you're worth the effort anymore.

Sometimes, buying yourself a brand-new outfit can help you feel sexy again. There is nothing wrong with splurging on yourself after a breakup, especially if it's going to make you feel better. If you see a pair of heels you love, BUY THEM. The smallest things that can make you smile and make you feel brand new again, are things you should invest in.

Don't let one bad breakup destroy you. You are stronger than you think. Picking yourself back up is one way you'll find your way back to who you used to be.

CHAPTER 6
The Chase

"The thing is, *I've tried* to move on. I've tried to forget his face, his touch, his laugh but every time I hear his name, all the memories come flashing back. I know he's done me wrong. He's broken my heart more than once but I just can't seem to forget him. And all I do is lie to everybody and pretend I'm over him. The reality is, he haunts my mind, day and night, and that's because I don't want to let him go… *not just yet*."

Do you keep trying harder to make things work or do you walk away for good? That's a decision that only YOU can make. I've been through a couple of relationships where I tried, and tried, and tried some more to make things work but at the end of the day, I knew I had to make the best decision for my heart, my soul AND my sanity to leave. It's never easy to walk away because you keep wondering how life will be without that person but it's also a losing battle if you end up fighting for your relationship alone.

A man that wants to be with you will show you. He won't play foolish head games.

I've been in this situation a few times, and so have many of my friends, where we believe our ex is trying to send us mixed messages or some kind of hidden clue that we need to decipher. BUT, *it's all in your head*. No ~~boy~~ man that wants to be with you, will play silly games to win your love. He won't have time for that type of foolishness because he'll be more invested in trying to woo you, and too busy trying to prove he can be fully trusted.

Sometimes, the woman makes it her quest to convince the man that he needs to be with her. She does whatever it takes to prove to him that she's loyal, worthy, honest... that she's the total package. She goes out of her way to send mixed signals to her ex so he can hopefully see that she is what his heart truly desires. This is a common mistake that we make and the worst is when our ex doesn't show signs that he feels the same way.

What I'm trying to convey to you is that you should never chase your ex, no matter how bad you want to be with him. It's normal to miss him. It's normal to want to be around him or know what he is up to, but when you start to *stalk* him or manipulate certain situations to try to catch his attention, it's NOT healthy.

The moment you start texting him or sending him funny or sexy memes, or even show up to places you know he usually hangs out in, is the moment you should start questioning your integrity.

Rather than just cut your losses, you persist in trying to show your ex how *valuable* you are to his life and why he needs you in it. You fail to realize that your advances might go unnoticed.

Do you believe he will value someone that keeps throwing themselves at him? Yes, there are some guys that will gladly take up your offer to get some booty, but that doesn't mean he's interested. That's NOT a sign that he wants to reconcile the relationship with you either.

The truth hurts? Yes, it does.

There were many occasions where I chased after my ex. I was blind then and didn't realize that all I was to him was a booty call. *Nothing more, nothing less*. He claimed we were best friends and claimed he cared, but I guess a part of him enjoyed the company more than anything. No commitment was good for him.

While I thought the time we spent together, hanging out was a step towards something meaningful, he was busy trying to meet other people on the side because he knew he had no attachment to me whatsoever. And I couldn't blame him because he made it clear on several occasions but I chose not to listen.

Instead, I chose to chase after him like a puppy dog, doing everything he wanted because in my little head, I believed that was bringing me one step closer to *getting back together with him*.

It's ludicrous to keep doing things repeatedly in hopes that you'll get a different result. You're overdoing it by chasing your ex because you keep imagining a perfect relationship with him when the truth is, you're no longer together and chances are, you might never be together again. So, to keep going back, trying to change his mind, will drive you insane.

I'm not against the idea of reconciliation, but I will always be against the idea of putting your ex before your happiness.

Chasing your ex can also be perceived as a sign of desperation and neediness. And those are signs you never want anybody to assume about you. Ask yourself why you truly want to get back with your ex, and the answer "I still love him" isn't good enough.

You should be asking yourself why would you want to take someone back who walked out on you and why would you try to start a new relationship with the same person that tore your heart into pieces. Or better yet, why would you want to be with someone who has made it obvious that they don't want to be with you?

I said it before, it's normal to miss your ex and feel miserable without them but remember that chasing them at this point is only going to cause you more grief than happiness.

Getting back together with someone who is toxic to your life is a sign that you don't think much of yourself because you'd rather be with someone that causes you agony, than be with someone new that can provide you with everything you desire. BUT, if your only reason to get back with your ex is because you BOTH want to give your relationship another try, go right ahead. There's nothing wrong in giving someone a second chance, as long as it's not the 4th, 5th, 6th, 7th...

They say cold turkey is the perfect way to stop smoking, well I say minimum of 30 days without contacting your ex is a great way to start anew. I know, from personal experience, that ignoring and avoiding all contact with your ex is a step towards the right direction. So instead of running after their love, you're busy running after a new beginning… a new start.

When one of my ex's and I broke up, we still spent time together hanging out because we missed that comfort, that feeling we once shared.

We ended up getting back together because we loved each other and we believed it was the right approach to healing. It was a total mistake and we should have left things broken because this time around, there was anger and bitterness that came with our last breakup. Everything that followed was unexpected because it felt as if we hated each other.

Because of this, I realized that sometimes, things are better off broken. You can't always try to put the pieces back together again because they might end up breaking into smaller pieces, which can create bigger issues.

So, when I tell you to take some time, stop chasing, unfollow them on social media, block their number and most of all, think about your wants and needs, it's because I know what it feels like to chase someone that just isn't worth the fight anymore.

Remind yourself that your heart is extremely vulnerable at this point and it will play tricks on you, so be cautious and *listen to your mind*, not your heart.

CHAPTER 7
He's Talking To Someone New

"You moved on so easily, and I can't be mad at her because she doesn't know all the bullshit you put me through. I hope she makes you smile the way *I once did*. I hope she's a better woman than what I was to you. I hope you find what you're looking for each time you look into her eyes but most of all, I hope she never becomes another victim in your web of lies because nobody deserves to have their heart broken by the person they truly love… *nobody.*"

Let me make it clear that when I write "...I hope she's a better woman than what I was to you.", I'm being sarcastic. I was a great woman to my ex, and he knows it to this day but I wish him and his partner well. I wanted to clarify this because some ladies might take the quote the wrong way and might not see the sarcasm behind it.

Now, this situation has occurred to many of us and if it hasn't, then you're a lucky one.

After a breakup, you feel as though the wounds are still fresh and there is no way that he could replace you. You believe that he is hurting the same way you are, but sometimes, it's quite the contrary. He's moved on with someone new, and that person is preoccupying his time so you're the last thing on his mind. You've heard through the grapevine that he is into her, and isn't afraid to show her off either.

The sound of your heart breaks because all you wonder is how he could betray you that way. How is he able to move forward with his life while you are still out here suffering and thinking about him 24/7? It doesn't make sense, right?

Once a man has moved on with his life, and is clearly showing you that he is no longer interested in what you once had, there is nothing holding him back from meeting someone new. It is never a good feeling when you feel you've been replaced. It hurts. It stings but the answer is also staring you right in the face, *he doesn't want you anymore*. The thing is, we sometimes choose not to accept that they've moved on without us.

During a breakup, you feel that you are still entitled to things you were entitled to when you were in a relationship, but fail to see that things are over. This is a hard pill to swallow for some because they would rather create an illusion of how they would like things to be instead of facing reality. So, it's quite normal that when our ex moves on, we feel a way about it because we feel he owes it to us to show us respect by not dating anybody else.

My ex did this to me and I can easily say, I wanted to punch him in the face. I couldn't understand how he could move on so quickly without thinking about my feelings. Is he that heartless that he couldn't care less about what

I'm going through? In my case, he was careless with my heart and didn't care one bit.

We broke up, and he jumped into a new relationship within 3 weeks (might have been sooner since he always lied). I was devastated because I still felt as if there was something between us. I couldn't understand how someone that claimed to love me could do me so wrong by dating someone new while I was still out here hurting. I blamed him for everything after that because I felt I needed to shed blame somewhere, for all the pain I was feeling.

The thing is, when someone breaks your heart, you don't forget them with a snap of a finger. You hold on to what you once had dearly and hold on to hope that someday, you might be reunited. When they bring a new woman into their lives and you see her doing all the things you used to do with him, it shatters you. Part of it is jealousy while another part is reminiscing on what you once shared. You ask yourself if he's forgotten all the *good times* you shared together or if he still reminisces about you, the same way you do.

A breakup means just that, a BREAK UP… broken… torn… no longer together. It's hard to accept the term especially when you have history with that person. You know them better than they know themselves, so you're quick to get upset at the fact that someone new has *taken your place.* But it's no longer your place and once you start to accept it, you'll realize them moving on means nothing to you.

You can get upset all you want, but that won't change the fact that his heart is somewhere else. And getting mad at her is also pointless because you're wasting valuable time stalking her, trying to find out who she is, what she wears, where she works… for what? It won't change where his heart is. I know, I know... this sounds harsh and you're probably hating me right about now but you need to hear the truth and not have someone sugarcoat it.

If he wanted to be with you, he would still be there. If he isn't, he's no longer interested in holding your heart.

I went through this several times, and you know what? It never helped to find out who *she was*. It hurt even more to put a face on the woman that held his heart in the palm of her hands.

I don't know what your situation is but whether he cheated with this woman and she knew about you, or she didn't know you existed, or she is completely oblivious about who you are and the past you shared with him… there is no point in hurting yourself by trying to figure out what she has that you don't. There's no point in trying to sabotage their relationship either.

I did these things and it hurt me in the end because, not only did I waste my time worrying about everything THEY were doing, but I also failed to see all the stress I was putting on myself. I was sabotaging my own happiness because I was more concerned about what I would be missing out on instead of setting myself free.

There were days where I kept wondering what his new woman had over me. Was it her hair color that shined more than mine? Was it because she was thinner than me? Was it because she dressed differently? What did she have that I didn't? Why wasn't I enough for him? Too many questions and not enough answers. No point in hurting yourself wondering what she has that makes him want her more than you.

The worst thing you can do to yourself is wonder what he is doing with her and where they are going. Is he taking her to the same places he used to take you? Is he giving her your nickname? These are things that will drive you insane if you don't accept that *he is no longer in your life.*

On another note, don't make the same mistakes I made by trying to find out through his friends what your ex is up to and how much he cares for his new woman. Have some dignity and don't lower yourself where you feel you should lie and manipulate a situation just to get useless information. It's not only manipulative, but it's wrong because I'm sure if you were in a brand-new relationship and your ex did that to you, you would hate him for it. See, I didn't see a problem with that back then because I was young and naïve.

Now, I couldn't care less what my ex is up to because I'm happy and successful, and he had no part in it so why bother wasting time thinking about him?

Now, while I don't agree that anybody should move on quickly, I do believe there is a period after a breakup to heal. And if your ex was willing to move on with someone new, chances are she's a rebound, he's already healed from your breakup or he's simply trying to move forward with his life with someone he genuinely cares about.

Either way, avoid stressing over someone that probably doesn't even know you exist or doesn't even care. It's not worth it especially when you're invisible in their eyes. So, anything you do won't affect them. Why waste your time?

CHAPTER 8
Healing Process

"There's so much strength in knowing *you're not okay* and you might not be for a while. Take all the time you need to heal. *There's no rush.*"

The one question I get frequently asked is "When will my heart stop hurting?" or "When does the pain go away?", and unfortunately, I have no right or wrong answer for that.

Healing doesn't happen overnight, and once you start accepting that, you'll find it easier to move forward. The longer you dwell on how long it'll take you to heal, the longer you'll stay stuck hoping to someday move on. Rushing it will only make things worse.

The pain will eventually pass. Everybody heals differently so *my pain isn't your pain*. I can tell you it'll pass within a few days, but that would be a lie. Some people heal within a few years, I'm the perfect example of that, while others heal within a few weeks or months. But, one thing I do know is that pain and hurt will eventually fade, and even though you might think about them every now and then, you'll also remember the pain you never want to feel again.

I haven't had many relationships but the few that I have had, have lasted a long period of time. The heartbreaks were different for each

one and some took longer to heal than others.
My ex was the hardest. It took me years to get over the heartbreak. Even though we weren't together, we kept in constant contact and that's what made it harder to let go.

We would hang out as friends, but sleep together as lovers. It was like having the best of both worlds, even though I knew it wasn't helping me heal from the fact that we were no longer together. We acted as if *being friends with benefits* was the right thing but it wasn't... and we knew it deep inside.

I knew that if we stopped talking or seeing each other, I would still have him on my mind. The thing that I failed to accept was the fact that he was always ready to move on without me. At the first opportunity, he could meet someone that he liked, he would drop me in a second because I was more of a distraction in his eyes... someone he could rely on to have a good time but at the same time, not commit to me because he liked me better in the *friendzone*.

Either way, I would always end up losing because I still hadn't healed from the original breakup and was covering it up by playing make-belief of what I wished our relationship would still be like.

All of this to say, if you don't take the necessary time to heal your wounds and keep covering them up with Band-Aids, you'll never fully mend your broken heart. You'll keep relapsing and it'll take longer and longer to move on.

One of the things you should never do is lie to yourself that you're *over him*. Sometimes, we tell ourselves "I'm great now. I'm better off without him." Or "I don't miss him at all. He's a jerk.". But you'll find little things that trigger your emotions and make you burst into tears because they remind you of *him*. Pretending that you're over him will only bring you more heart ache because you haven't fully accepted what you're truly feeling.

Listening to your friends can sometimes hinder your healing process especially if they were friends with your ex too.

You all share a history and a mutual friend

might bring up good times you all shared. That can easily affect how you feel, and might even make you want to burst out in tears because the good memories you once shared are a thing of the past... something you won't ever get back.

That's the thing with the healing process. It doesn't happen with a blink of an eye. It's a process which doesn't mean you're broken, it simply means it's a long process especially when it's over someone you deeply loved.

One thing I found amusing throughout some of my breakups was the fact that some of my friends would automatically assume that me crying was because I wanted my ex back. That wasn't the case. They failed to realize that we shared years together, and even though I was in a better place and I had my life back on track, there were moments where I felt vulnerable. There were moments where I felt the need to let it all out. And there is nothing wrong with letting a cry out, every now and then. It's very beneficial to let all those emotions out.

It might happen, out of the blue, that you feel a load of feelings taking over your body and you can't fully understand why. You're human. It's normal if you end up turning into a ball of tears. Shit happens, and sometimes it's out of your control. You'll feel things, at certain points of your life, because they get triggered by past moments you once shared with a person you once cared deeply for. And it's okay, so don't let anybody tell you otherwise. You're not made of stone so it's okay to cry, it's okay to be mad, it's okay to be confused.

Healing comes in different stages. You can't rush it. You can't give it a timeline. There is no magic potion for it either, so letting things flow and take their course is necessary. Here are my 6 stages to the healing process after a breakup (some people have more, some people have less but these are the stages that have helped me in the past):

Shock

You don't know what just happened and you're in a state of disbelief. You're trying to comprehend why things happened the way they did, or even if what's happening is true. A part of you feels as though everything you're going through is a dream… a nightmare, and you can't seem to wake up. An unexpected breakup can cause you to feel many emotions and being in shock is natural. You can't believe it. Everything is gone. Everything you shared is over.

You have trouble sleeping and keep replaying the breakup in your head because it's something you weren't expecting. Whatever you do, don't freak out. It's normal for you to feel the way you're feeling. Eventually it will all make sense.

I know what it feels like to be fixated on things your ex said during the breakup. It sometimes feels as though things he said contradict the breakup, and you want answers. Your mind swings back and forth in disbelief of everything going on. It's never a pleasant feeling.

And then, you have moments of clarity where you accept what is happening to you. It's as if your heart and mind are a yo-yo, and all you're doing is going up and down… up and down.

I know, you fought hard to keep the relationship alive to the point where you lost yourself in the process. So, to think that it's ending is quite shocking because you expected it to last forever. The idea of living without that person feels unbearable but you know what?

YOU WILL BE OKAY.

Denial

This phase is a tough one because you end up believing everything your heart is saying instead of believing what your mind is telling you.

"IT JUST CAN'T BE TRUE!"

There's no way that your ex is no longer going to be a part of your life. There's no way that he can just leave you when you've invested time and effort into building the relationship to what it is now. There's no way you're losing him.

It's a tough thing to admit to ourselves that the person we loved no longer wants to be with us, and denial after a breakup is one of the hardest things you'll go through because it's sometimes just too painful to face the truth.

The longer you take to accept that he is no longer with you, the longer it'll take you to work towards healing. You'll derail the grieving process by replacing it with hope that you can make things work… even though he's clearly showed you signs that he's no longer interested in building a future with you.

Trying to salvage something that is no longer there is simply creating false expectations of how you wished things would turn out. Entertaining fantasies of things *working out* are things you do when you're in denial.

Accepting what is happening, even though it hurts, is the only way you'll move on to the next phase, closer to healing.

Bargaining

This phase usually goes hand in hand with denial. You're willing to do anything to avoid accepting it's over, and you're willing to change things (that probably didn't need to be changed) to keep the relationship alive. You'll try to do whatever it takes to get him back, and that's never a good sign.

When you tell him that you're willing to compromise your happiness or promise to be a better person if your ex will take you back, that's a sign that you're not being realistic with your expectations.

Bargaining is a form of negotiation which can also sometimes include subtle threats. Telling your ex that him leaving is going to cause damage to your kids or that you might end your life, are horrible ways to try to mend something that should remain broken.

Now, don't get me wrong, I'm not saying that you shouldn't work hard at making things work if you have children. On the contrary, I'm the first one to push couples that have a family into therapy, or whatever way that can help mend the broken pieces to your relationship BUT when you know deep within that things aren't meant to be, there's a fine line where you should let things go and move on.

All bargaining does is push you further into believing that your fantasy is real, when it's obviously not. You're not logical when you believe you can win him back at any cost. If you're constantly trying to force or beg someone to love you, it's NOT love. It's a fantasy of how you want things to be.

Bargaining is also a way of inflicting pain onto yourself because you're taking blame for everything that happened and you're willing to risk everything to make things right. You're willing to do anything except accept the fact that it's over.

Clinging to hope and promising to fix all the problems you're both having is also placing a burden in trying to repair something that might be irreparable, and sustaining the entire relationship by yourself. It's as if you're accepting to take responsibility for everything that happens here on out. Now, why would you place such a burden on yourself alone?

It's NOT your responsibility to maintain the relationship by yourself. A relationship is based on the effort of two people, not one.

Relapse

Oh my! Oh my! Been through this a few times and it never ends well. We want a happy ending and assume our ex can give it to us.

The pain without them seems intolerable so you do your best to find ways to convince your ex to give it another try. The thing is, if you've already done the *back and forth thing*, you should ask yourself "how long will it last this time?"

Most people that relapse end up going back and forth with their relationship, believing next time will be different.

When you relapse, you sometimes end up making things worse because you might end up bringing up the reasons you originally broke up or bring up situations that bothered you while you were apart. All you're really doing is patching up the pieces and relieving the agony of withdrawal.

Despite your best efforts, things might not work out the way you want them to. While you think you're doing the right thing by going back to the arms of the person that broke your heart because you're comfortable or you're simply accustomed to them, you might end up signing your own heartbreak once again.

Chances are you might go through the process of breaking up and making back up again, more than once, before you finally realize, *it's over*.

Anger

Anger is the stage I couldn't stand the most because it became frustrating and confusing, all in one. I went from missing someone to hating them, or somewhat close to it.

Your thoughts start to wander and all you keep asking yourself is why things are happening to you. You become upset because the effects of denial begin to die down, and the thought of what your ex did to you fuels you with anger.

The thought of him makes you want to slander his name, burn pictures of the both of you or even hold his things hostage because... well... *it just feels good* to piss him off. He broke your heart so why not do something that makes *you* feel better? I know, I've been there but at the end of it all, I realized that all I was doing was trying to place blame somewhere.

And no matter how much I tried to suppress my anger, I felt the need to blame someone for all the wrongdoing that was done to me. This made me direct my anger at anyone that crossed my path, even if they didn't merit it. If I was mad, well others were going to feel my wrath too. This is something you'll have to learn to control or the anger will consume you.

All you're doing is suppressing emotional issues. You're upset at your ex for his betrayal, for breaking your heart, for his lack of emotions but you don't know what else to do to get your point across. Once you feel anger, it can be an empowering moment because you're justifying that you deserve more than what your ex was willing to give you, and realizing this is a great step towards the right direction.

Don't settle for the type of love you're given if you know it's not the type of love you want, or the type of you are owed. YOU matter.

Acceptance

This stage is where you start to feel more like yourself again because you learn to accept why you were with him, why you're not, and you know that things will be okay. You come to terms with the loss of your relationship while knowing that you're better off without them.

Acceptance is the best medicine to healing because you're finally able to exhale, and you're excited for the future. You're ready to move on with your life because you know that even though you might still have feelings of regret or guilt, you've accepted the reality of your situation. You know it's over. You know your ex is no longer a part of your life (in the case of children involved, the same applies only that you know they're no longer a part of YOUR life, only a part of YOUR CHILDREN's lives).

Learning to be alone and being able to live an independent life, is the right approach to healing and knowing that your life will be okay without them.

All these stages are part of the healing process, but always remember that TIME is the only thing that will help you push forward. I know it may not be the answer that you've been meaning to hear but it's an honest one. Nothing happens overnight and the moment you start to accept it, you'll realize that *better days are coming*.

CHAPTER 9
No Stress.
Live Again.

"I no longer dwell on what could have been.
I focus on the present and how good I'm
going without you. My mind wanders, from
time to time, on the memories we once shared
but then I remind myself why we're no longer
together. What we once had is gone,
and I'm finally okay with that."

A common mistake we make after a break up is to let stress take over our bodies and allow it to ruin our lives.

Friends and family will tell you to move on as if it's as easy as a 1-2-3, but the truth of the matter is, they mean it because *they love you*. They want what's best for you and want to make sure that you're okay. So, as obnoxious as they may sound, understand that they mean well. Some might tell you to relax and live life and as hard as that may seem, you can do it!

Stress is our worst enemy. And when we allow it to consume us, we become miserable. Here are a few steps I've taken to release the stress:

Change your thoughts

If you start thinking of things that stress you out, shift your thought process to something that makes you smile and laugh. Every time I felt stress coming on, I thought of the gym. It was my other home and became more of a hobby at some point, but it definitely helped to relieve the stress I was putting on myself.

Take a deep breath

This might sound silly to some but using a deep breathing technique helps to alleviate stress in many ways.

I tried the 4-7-8 technique and it helped me enormously to unwind, and not constantly add unnecessary stress to my life. The good thing is you can do this anywhere, without the need of any equipment.

1. You can either keep your hands to your sides, or you can put one hand on your belly and another on your chest, then exhale through your mouth.

2. Close your mouth and take a deep, slow breath from your belly while mentally counting to 4.

3. Hold your breath and count to 7.

4. Exhale completely, through your mouth, while counting to 8.

5. Now, repeat these steps 3 to 7 more times, until you feel calm.

Write two lists

One thing I did that helped relieve my stress was writing everything, that was stressing me out, on a piece of paper. I wrote down everything and I literally mean E-V-E-R-Y-T-H-I-N-G that made my heart turn upside down. I made two lists to simplify everything.

The first list I wrote was the root causes of my stress while the second one was the actions on how to address them.

Once I had everything written down, I re-read it a couple of times and made it my goal to complete the action tasks. I visualized myself utilizing and depleting all the stress I built up. And within a few weeks, I accomplished everything I set out to do. Round of applause.

Imagine your life in the future

This might be a tough thing to do for some of you especially if you're fixated on your ex. But it works if you're willing to put in the effort.

Imagine your life five years from now, then imagine ten years later, then twenty, and so forth. As you think further into the future, you'll start to see that many things you're worried about now aren't as important as you think. There are bigger things to worry about than someone that broke your heart and the further into the future you go, the better you'll feel because you'll eventually realize that you're good without the person that broke your heart.

Laugh, and laugh some more

Laughing is the cure to many things but it soothes any type of tension you might be going through and eases the pain, even for a little while. You may not want to laugh because of all the hardships you're going through but laughing is the remedy you're looking for.

Even if you only have a few minutes to spare, put on a funny video or movie that you know will bring a smile to your face. Any type of laughter is better than no laughter at all, and it's great for your immune system, so why not give it a try?

All these steps might not be suitable for all of you but if you at least give one of them a try, I'm sure you'll feel some sense of relaxation. Letting stress go and living again is a great way to overcome any sadness or anger you're feeling.

CHAPTER 10
Never Give Up On The Good Guy

"Someday, the *right man* will find me. I'm no longer scared of waiting because I know no matter how long it takes, he will do right by me. *It will be worth the wait.*"

I wasn't going to include this chapter in the book because I touched part of it in the previous volume but I figured there was more to say on the topic.

THERE ARE LOTS OF GOOD MEN OUT THERE!

Yes, yes, I can hear some of you saying "Well, where are they?" or "Nah, they don't exist.", but the truth of the matter is if you're not running across any of these good guys, there's something you might be doing wrong.

It's quite possible that he's standing right in front of your face and you don't even notice him. We sometimes become so consumed with how our ex was, that we try to find someone that's similar to them because that's what we are used to. And I'm not saying there's something wrong with your choice of men but maybe the type of guys you're going after are the same ones that will keep breaking your heart. You can't keep looking for your past in all the new guys you meet, and you can't expect that they will all hurt you because that is definitely not the case. Maybe it's time to try something new, a different approach.

A perfect example is looking for a guy at a bar or club. You want someone fun and exciting, I get that. But that doesn't necessarily mean you'll meet the type of guy that's interested in a serious long-term relationship in a place like that.

Some men in those environments are into one thing only, and that's who they can take home for the night. If that's not what you're looking for, stop meeting guys there. Look elsewhere.

There's also the possibility that you have the *good guy* right in front of you but you ignore him because he's missing a quality or two that you're accustomed to. I've heard many of my male friends complain about women being *gold-diggers* and not wanting anything serious if they weren't able to *provide* for them. So, in other words, you would prefer a jerk that treats you like sh*t but buys you everything over someone that has a less-paying job, and is totally head over heels in love with you?

I don't get it.

The good guy is right there, but you keep overlooking him because you're probably assuming he's boring or weak instead of giving him a chance to impress you.

Throughout the years, I've noticed that women with low self-esteem will attract the "bad guys" because they feel that is all they deserve. If you don't think much of yourself, you'll keep reinforcing that negative belief and will keep going from one toxic relationship to the next. It becomes a vicious cycle when you stop believing "good guys" exist.

A *bad guy* can sense the insecurity in you, and knows when you feel you're not worthy enough of *his* love. He knows when you believe you're not "pretty enough" too, so when the opportunity arises, he will say all the right things to woo you and once he's got you trapped... you can say goodbye to whatever is left of your self-esteem.

You will never find your worth in a man because your worth can only be found within yourself. And that's when you'll find a man who's worthy of you!

Another thing I've noticed is whenever a man becomes attentive to your needs and shows you effort, wanting to spend time with you, showing you clear signs that he wants to get to know you better, you push him away because you feel he's being *too nice*. Or there's also the type of woman that is used to controlling her men, she will lose respect for the *nice guy* because she feels he is doing *too much*, and isn't letting her control everything. Sound odd? Very, but it's a proven fact that many women will react this way because they want to be the one to call the shots.

What I'm trying to show you here is that not all men are bad, and not all men are good either. The fact that many of you have been through bad relationships and also witness the same *bad relationships* over your TV screens, Internet and so forth, have conditioned you to believe the worst may happen with your current relationship. It's a never-ending battle with yourself because you keep believing that *nice guys* don't exist… when they do.

So, if the right one comes along, don't let him go. You just never know where you might end up a few years down the line.

CHAPTER 11
New Beginnings

"You won't stay heartbroken forever.
The day will come when you feel a sense of relief in knowing you're no longer attached to the person that once broke you. All the overthinking and pain you once felt will be a thing of the *past*. You'll remember the good times you once shared but you'll also remember the agony you went through, and that will push you to be *stronger* and *wiser* towards future relationships. You'll never allow anybody to ever treat you like a puppet again."

YOU WILL SURVIVE! I mean that with the best intentions, because I know firsthand what it feels like to have your heart ripped out your chest and feel as though nobody understands what you're going through.

When I look back at my past relationships, I see growth. They have shaped me into the woman I am today and I am proud of how far I've come. The same applies to you. After everything you've been through, you deserve a happy ending. You deserve to be treated with the utmost respect and deserve someone that is willing to show you consistency.

Starting over can be scary, *I know*. It's never an easy task to start something new and never easy to say goodbye to your past, but you've got to keep reminding yourself that you are allowed to be happy! You are allowed to feel love again, even if it's not with the same person you imagined it with.

Every mistake you've ever made is considered a valuable lesson. It gives you the opportunity to grow. It shows you your values. It teaches you that not everything will always go as planned but even though these *mistakes* hurt, they will push you to become a better version of yourself. Every experience teaches you something new so never feel as though the world is against you because it's giving you the chance to re-evaluate your life.

Whenever something bad happens, you should ask yourself what you have learned from that experience. It might not be pleasant to accept it but the truth of the matter is you'll learn to not repeat the same mistakes, again and again.

Your mistakes don't define or represent who you are as a person. Accepting that you're much more than your problems is a great sign of growth.

I can assure you that it's normal to be afraid to make future mistakes and to also be afraid of taking that leap, *to jump*, out of fear of failure. We've all been in situations during our life where we're unsure if we should take a risk or lose it all. I've been in that situation a few times but each time, I took a plunge because I didn't want to live my life with regret. It hasn't been a bed of roses each time but I knew that even if it ended up being a mistake, I had taken that jump… and it felt damn good! So, if you find you're holding yourself back from reaching your goals or meeting someone new, you're probably worried of making a mistake. But without those mistakes, there would be no growth, and no growth would mean you'd always stay stuck in the same place. Life is a gamble, never forget that.

Everything you thought would break you, *didn't*.

Instead of harboring resentment or blaming others, you can take this new beginning by embracing your emotions. Think about the emotional rollercoaster you've survived and think about how far you've come to be where you are standing now. Be thankful for the experience, and thankful that you're no longer in that situation.

No matter how challenging life gets, you know you've been through a storm. You stuck through it, even when it was extremely painful, and pushed through like a warrior. You didn't let the anger and pain get to you. You grew stronger with this experience and made wise choices that pushed you towards the path of positivity. Unfortunately, some weren't as lucky as you. They failed when push came to shove, and never learned anything from their downfall. They let the pain take over, and stayed stuck in a rut. If I had let my emotions invade my thoughts after any one of my break ups, I wouldn't be where I am today. So, even though you may believe you haven't accomplished anything after your breakup, you're dead wrong. You've gained wisdom and strength in knowing that after any downfall, you should pick yourself back up even stronger than the last time.

Sometimes, you must *lose yourself* to find yourself again. That should propel you to see life differently. You'll love yourself unconditionally because you know the one person you'll always be able to rely on is *you*. Starting over doesn't mean you're forgetting your past, you're just tucking it far far away in your head to make space for better things... better people.

A new beginning means there is a light at the end of the tunnel. There is no magic potion on where to begin or any secrets to starting over. I've given you several scenarios throughout the book on how to move forward with your life but just to do a quick recap, here are a few steps you should follow before starting anew:

- Clear the way from your past loves. In other words, separate yourself emotionally from your loss. A physical separation due to a death or a breakup is never the same as an emotional separation.

- Grieve the loss you've gone through. Some people can grieve for a few days, while some of us may take a few months or years. No matter the amount of time, take as much time as you need as long as it helps you let go.

- Mourn your loss as if it was a death, even though your partner is still alive. The same way you're *dying inside* is the same way you should feel about your ex. You have to get it through your head that this is no longer a *breakup*, a *separation*. This is the death of your relationship. This is goodbye.

- Let your emotions flow. Whether it's anger, sadness, loneliness, etc, let them out and feel them fully.

- Learn to be alone, and enjoy the time you spend with yourself. There is nothing more gratifying than knowing you are your best company and you don't need anybody else to feel complete.

- Live again! Live your life to the fullest. Enjoy the good weather, go on trips, go out with friends, experience something new. Being single doesn't mean the end.

- Focus on being a better you, which also means taking care of yourself. Take care of your career and your future goals, put your focus on the things you want to accomplish.

- Move on. Let go. *Once you're ready*, you'll know when to start something serious with a new love interest.

Keep reminding yourself that if your past relationship didn't work out, it wasn't a waste. Everything happened for a reason and it prepared you to become the person you are today. Your choices are what led you to this breakthrough. There's nothing greater than moving on and succeeding, that's the best revenge. Instead of wallowing in your pain, use the strength you have deep within you to pick yourself back up and move past all your hardships.

Every step you've taken is a step towards something bigger, and that's something to smile about!

Now, exhale and keep pushing forward, never backwards.

"If it's meant to be, you will find your way back to one another… but you shouldn't stop your life waiting for something that may never happen."

"I should hate you for all you've done to me. I wouldn't wish that pain on anybody. You go around living your life as if you've done nothing wrong, but the truth is, you're *selfish*. All you ever cared about were your feelings, your wants, your needs. I was just a pawn in your game of lies. And even though I know I'll never get the apology I deserve, I *forgive you* because I owe it to myself to heal and I owe it to myself to move on."

"I learned to live without you but I never forgot you. That's the funny thing about love because it took me a long time to forgive and forget the pain you caused, but a piece of you always remains within me. I couldn't brush off all the good memories we shared and sweep them under the rug as if they meant nothing. So, I put you in a safe place for new memories to be built with *someone new*. You see, I deserve to be happy again, even if it's not with you. And even though I might reminisce about us every now and then, it doesn't mean I miss you. It simply means I haven't forgotten who *you used to be*."

The End

Your Notes

Your Notes

Instagram
www.instagram.com/sweetzthoughts

Facebook
www.facebook.com/sweetzthoughts

The Mistakes Of A Woman -
Volume 2: New Beginnings (2017)